UMOREN KOKO

Hebrews 11:1 – KJV
Now faith is the substance of things hoped
for, the evidence of things not seen.

UNDERSTANDING

FAITH

UMOREN KOKO

ISBN   978-978-59058-3-0

Copyright © Umoren Koko 2023

All scriptures are taken from the King James Version of the Bible. This version was preferred because it is an earlier version than most of the other versions of the Bible in circulation.

Many other versions are basically interpretations and translations of the KJV. Therefore, to avoid this work being influenced by a third party's interpretation or translation, the KJV became the preferred Bible.

CONTENTS

DEDICATION

This book is dedicated to you the reader.

INTRODUCTION

Before we attempt to understand the concept of faith, we need to establish how important this topic is. There are two importance of faith recorded in the bible, and they are 1) To please God 2) to move mountains.

Hebrew 11:6 - KJV

6. But without faith it is impossible to please him: for he that cometh to God must believe that he is, and that he is a rewarder of them that diligently seek him.

Here we see that we need faith if we are to please God.

Matthew 17:20 - KJV

20. And Jesus said unto them, Because of your unbelief: for verily I say unto you, If ye have faith as a grain of mustard seed, **ye shall say unto this mountain, Remove hence to yonder place;** *and it shall remove; and nothing shall be impossible unto you.*

1 Corinthians 13:2 - KJV

20. And though I have the gift of prophecy, and understand all mysteries, and all knowledge; and though I have all faith, so that I could **remove mountains,** *and have not charity, I am nothing.*

The above passages show that faith can be used to remove mountains. The common misunderstanding with these two passages is that many think they were talking about physical mountains. But here they were using mountains to refer to obstacles and troubles and challenges that one might face at any point in time.

Therefore, you need faith to solve these challenges, obstacles, troubles, issues. No matter where they arise, be it in your career or your family or your relationships with people etc. you will always need faith to solve them.

Now, what then is faith?

FAITH

Circular meaning of faith

According to the dictionary, faith is defined as complete confidence in something.

Here I would like you to take note of the word "**complete**" and the word "**confidence**".

Please hold unto these two words in your mind.

Biblical meaning of faith

According to the bible, faith is defined as:

Hebrews 11:1 - KJV

1. Now faith is the substance of things hoped for, the evidence of things not seen.

Here I would like you to take note of the words "**substance**" and "**evidence**"

You also have to take note of the definition of faith in the book of Hebrew, it is telling us that faith is not hope, but the substance of the things we hope for. There is therefore a difference between faith and hope.

This definition also puts distance between faith and things that we have not seen but describes faith as the evidence of the things we have not seen.

Most times what we call faith is just us holding unto hopes and things that are unseen without any substance to our hopes or evidence to back up the unseen things we hold unto. According to Hebrew 11:1 if there is no substance or evidence, then it is not faith.

Substance:

Is the physical matter of which a person or thing consists and which has a tangible and solid presence.

This means that faith is not having hope in something but having physical and tangible proof/presence to represent your hope. This means hope becomes faith when you can use physical and tangible matter to prove it (to provide evidence).

Evidence:

Is the available body of facts or information, indicating whether a belief or proposition is true or valid.

This means that faith is not about holding onto things that are unseen but faith is to be able to provide facts or information to show that the unseen that you hold unto is true or valid.

Therefore, faith is not about having hopes or holding onto something unseen, but faith is about being able to back up your hopes and unseen things with substance and evidence. But to provide substance or evidence to anything, you must possess an understanding of that thing.

Therefore, if there is no faith without substance and evidence, there is no faith without understanding. This means that if you can't have faith without being able to provide substance and evidence, you can't have faith in something you do not understand.

To prove that Jesus had faith, he was always able to provide substance and evidence to his teachings using real-life things as parables. He was always able to explain how his teachings affect real life. This showed that he truly understood the things he was talking about. In other words, Jesus had faith (complete confidence) in what he was talking about.

The word evidence is taken from the word evident which means obvious to the eyes. Thus, you really can't have faith in something you haven't understood to a point where you can make it obvious to the eyes.

Many people have hope that the things they have heard are right but until they can provide evidence or substance to their belief systems, all they have is hope, not faith.

Faith can't exist without these two words "Substance" and "evidence".

"Substance" and "evidence" can't exist without "understanding".

Faith therefore can't exist without "understanding".

If we marry the conventional definition of faith and the definition in Hebrew, this means that to have complete confidence in a person or something, you must have an understanding of that person or something. You can't have complete confidence in who/what you do not understand. It is simply impossible.

You can hope that a thing or a person will deliver for you, but you can't have complete confidence when you do not understand that thing or that person.

You can't go into an examination with complete confidence except you have an understanding of the subject matter.

If we take another look at the biblical definition of faith.

Hebrews 11:1 - KJV

1. Now faith is the substance of things hoped for, the evidence of things not seen.

You can't give substance to things you hope for except you have understood those things.

You can't provide evidence to things unseen except you have understood them.

The summary here is that faith is standing on a foundation called understanding.

Faith = Understanding.

FAITH AND

RIGHTEOUSNESS

One of the uses of faith that we discussed earlier is that faith is what is needed to please God. And to please God is the same thing as being righteous.

Hebrew 11:6 - KJV

6. But without faith it is impossible to please him: for he that cometh to God must believe that he is, and that he is a rewarder of them that diligently seek him.

David in the bible was one man who seemed to know the secret to righteousness.

Psalms 111:10 – KJV

*10.   The fear of the LORD is the beginning of wisdom: a good **understanding** have all they that do his commandments: his praise endureth for ever.*

Psalms 119:34 – KJV

*34.   Give me **understanding,** and I shall keep thy law; yea, I shall observe it with my whole heart.*

David seems to believe that the secret ingredient to keeping the commandments of God and pleasing God is understanding.

The author of Hebrew says it is Faith.

Once again, we are faced with the conclusion that Faith = Understanding.

In the first place, it is difficult to please a person that you do not understand. Be it your spouse, your boss, or anyone, you can't please them without understanding them. It's the same with God.

Also, you can't have faith in whom you do not understand.

When it comes to keeping the commandments of God, many people struggle to do so simply because they have not understood the commandments and why they exist., many people have not understood that the commandments of God are for their own good, not God's.

A good example is someone who lies and does not realise that it is his own reputation and credibility at stake, not God's.

Another example is fornication. People who disobey this do not fully grasp the consequences of their actions both to their soul and their body. God will never be at risk of any sexually transmitted disease. It is the fornicator at risk. God is never at risk of a broken marriage or relationship or broken heart. It is always the perpetrator of fornication or adultery.

There are other things to understand that will help one stay righteous easily, but the basic understanding of this is that being righteous is not for God's benefit but Man's.

Many people think that the commandments are in place for God's benefit because of the way they have been taught. They do not understand that the only reason your unrighteousness displeases God, is because he loves you and can't stand watching the consequences you have to face because of your unrighteousness.

Man's inability to stay righteous and please God is simply down to lack of understanding (faith).

JESUS ON FAITH

Matthew 16:5-12 - KJV

5.   And when his disciples were come to the other side, they had forgotten to take bread.

6.   Then Jesus said unto them, Take heed and beware of the leaven of the Pharisees and of the Sadducees.

7.   And they reasoned among themselves, saying, It is because we have taken no bread.

8.   Which when Jesus perceived, he said unto them, O ye of little faith, why reason ye among yourselves, because ye have brought no bread?

9.   Do ye not yet understand, neither remember the five loaves of the five thousand, and how many baskets ye took up?

10. Neither the seven loaves of the four thousand, and how many baskets ye took up?

11.   How is it that ye do not understand that I spake it not to you concerning bread, that ye should beware of the leaven of the Pharisees and of the Sadducees?

12.   Then understood they how that he bade them not beware of the leaven of bread, but of the doctrine of the Pharisees and of the Sadducees.

In this story, Jesus and his disciples had moved from one place to another when they realized that they had forgotten to take food (bread).

Then he warned them to be careful of the leaven of the Pharisees but they automatically thought he was talking about collecting bread from the Pharisees.

When he perceived that this is what the disciples were thinking, he called them "o ye of little faith".

8.   Which when Jesus perceived, he said unto them, O ye of little faith, why reason ye among yourselves, because ye have brought no bread?

But the key to this story is in how he begins verse 9. "Do ye not yet understand"

9.   Do ye not yet understand, neither remember the five loaves of the five thousand, and how many baskets ye took up?

He compared their lack of faith to a lack of understanding.

They had already seen him perform miracles with bread in the past. So definitely they should believe or at least hope that he would be able to provide them with bread. He was just disappointed that they did not understand that he was not talking about physical bread. He was just warning them not to take in the teachings and doctrines of the Pharisees.

10.   Neither the seven loaves of the four thousand, and how many baskets ye took up?

11.   How is it that ye do not understand that I spake it not to you concerning bread, that ye should beware of the leaven of the Pharisees and of the Sadducees?

*12.   Then understood they how that he bade them not beware of the leaven of bread, but of the **doctrine** of the Pharisees and of the Sadducees.*

Their failure to understand him is why he referred to them as people of little faith.

Like we said earlier it is impossible to have faith in what/whom you do not understand.

There is another story where Jesus used faith to imply understanding. This story is written in the book of Matthew, chapter 8.

Matthew 8:5-13 - KJV

5. And when Jesus was entered into Capernaum, there came unto him a centurion, beseeching him,

6. And saying, Lord, my servant lieth at home sick of the palsy, grievously tormented.

7. And Jesus saith unto him, I will come and heal him.

8. The centurion answered and said, Lord, I am not worthy that thou shouldest come under my roof: but speak the word only, and my servant shall be healed.

9. For I am a man under authority, having soldiers under me: and I say to this man, Go, and he goeth; and to another, Come, and he cometh; and to my servant, Do this, and he doeth it.

10. When Jesus heard it, he marvelled, and said to them that followed, Verily I say unto you, I have not found so great faith, no, not in Israel.

11. And I say unto you, That many shall come from the east and west, and shall sit down with Abraham, and Isaac, and Jacob, in the kingdom of heaven.

12. But the children of the kingdom shall be cast out into outer darkness: there shall be weeping and gnashing of teeth.

13. And Jesus said unto the centurion, Go thy way; and as thou hast believed, so be it done unto thee. And his servant was healed in the selfsame hour.

This story is about a man (a centurion; a captain in the army) from Capernaum. This man met Jesus on the way and pleaded with Jesus to help him heal his servant who was not present with him but at home. Then Jesus answered him and said that he (Jesus) would follow the centurion home. To which the centurion replied that Jesus didn't need to follow him to his house because the healing could be done from where they were irrespective of distance. This prompted Jesus to say that he had not seen such a faith in the whole of Israel.

So why did Jesus say this? The answer is simple, the centurion displayed a level of understanding that Jesus had not witnessed in Israel. This understanding was displayed in verses 8 and 9.

8. The centurion answered and said, Lord, I am not worthy that thou shouldest come under my roof: but speak the word only, and my servant shall be healed.

9. For I am a man under authority, having soldiers under me: and I say to this man, Go, and he goeth; and to another, Come, and he cometh; and to my servant, Do this, and he doeth it.

In these verses the centurion explains that because of his understanding of how authority works, and he sees Jesus to be a man of spiritual authority, then Jesus doesn't need to go all the way to his house. It was this understanding of spiritual authority that made his faith in Jesus higher compared to whatever Jesus had witnessed prior.

Many other people came there for healing and other miracles, usually they brought out their sick and waited for Jesus by the way, some even struggled to touch his garment. But this centurion was the first to believe that he didn't need to drag his sick servant along with him because he understood how authority works and he saw Jesus to be a man of spiritual authority. His level of understanding determined his level of faith.

There is another story in the book of mark which is even more intriguing than the ones we have discussed. In the book of Mark chapter 11, there are two stories where Jesus is teaching his disciples about faith. The first story occurs between verses 1 & 6.

Mark 11:1-6 - KJV

1. And when they came nigh to Jerusalem, unto Bethphage and Bethany, at the mount of Olives, he sendeth forth two of his disciples,

2. And saith unto them, Go your way into the village over against you: and as soon as ye be entered into it, ye shall find a colt tied, whereon never man sat; loose him, and bring him.

3. And if any man say unto you, Why do ye this? say ye that the Lord hath need of him; and straightway he will send him hither.

4. And they went their way, and found the colt tied by the door without in a place where two ways met; and they loose him.

5. And certain of them that stood there said unto them, What do ye, loosing the colt?

6. And they said unto them even as Jesus had commanded: and they let them go.

7. And they brought the colt to Jesus, and cast their garments on him; and he sat upon him.

8. And many spread their garments in the way: and others cut down branches off the trees, and strawed them in the way.

9. And they that went before, and they that followed, cried, saying, Hosanna; Blessed is he that cometh in the name of the Lord:

In this story, Jesus sends two disciples to go to a nearby village to untie a Colt (donkey) because he wanted to use it to ride into the city.

He tells them to untie the colt and bring it to him and if anyone asked them why they were taking a colt that didn't belonged to them, they should reply by saying "*the Lord hath need of him*".

This was a demonstration of faith but was grounded on understanding; an understanding of what to say if anyone asked why the disciples were taking the animal. If they had said any other thing, they could have been denied the colt or worst still they could have been called thieves.

Knowing what to say could have been due to divine knowledge or simply that Jesus understood the people of that village. Whichever one it was, it was the basis for the faith Jesus had that the colt would be released to the disciples.

The second story in this chapter starts from verse 11 to verse

Mark 11:11-22 - KJV

11. And Jesus entered into Jerusalem, and into the temple: and when he had looked round about upon all things, and now the eventide was come, he went out unto Bethany with the twelve.

12. And on the morrow, when they were come from Bethany, he was hungry:

13. And seeing a fig tree afar off having leaves, he came, if haply he might find any thing thereon:

and when he came to it, he found nothing but leaves; for the time of figs was not yet.

14. And Jesus answered and said unto it, No man eat fruit of thee hereafter for ever. And his disciples heard it.

15. And they come to Jerusalem: and Jesus went into the temple, and began to cast out them that sold and bought in the temple, and overthrew the tables of the moneychangers, and the seats of them that sold doves;

16. And would not suffer that any man should carry any vessel through the temple.

17. And he taught, saying unto them, Is it not written, My house shall be called of all nations the house of prayer? but ye have made it a den of thieves.

18. And the scribes and chief priests heard it, and sought how they might destroy him: for they feared him, because all the people was astonished at his doctrine.

19. And when even was come, he went out of the city.

20. And in the morning, as they passed by, they saw the fig tree dried up from the roots.

21. And Peter calling to remembrance saith unto him, Master, behold, the fig tree which thou cursedst is withered away.

22. And Jesus answering saith unto them, Have faith in God.

In this story, Jesus curses a fig tree that had no fruit for him and his disciples. Take note that Jesus only did this to teach his disciples an important lesson of faith. I say this because even Jesus was aware that it was not the season for the fig tree to have fruits, therefore the tree was in its right not to have fruits.

13. And seeing a fig tree afar off having leaves, he came, if haply he might find any thing thereon: and when he came to it, he found nothing but leaves; **for the time of figs was not yet.**

But still Jesus cursed the tree saying "*No man eat fruit of thee hereafter for ever*". But something strange happened the next day, the tree had dried up.

20. And in the morning, as they passed by, they saw the fig tree dried up from the roots.

21. And Peter calling to remembrance saith unto him, Master, behold, the fig tree which thou cursedst is withered away.

Take note that Jesus never said to the tree that it should dry up or wither away but yet this was the result of the cure he pronounced on the tree. Perhaps this was actually the end goal of Jesus but he understood exactly how to get it done.

He could have just said to the tree to dry up but perhaps the tree would refuse to dry up because it still had reason to be alive (producing figs in its season for people to consume). By saying *"No man eat fruit of thee hereafter for ever"*, Jesus was disconnecting the tree from its purpose thereby taking away its will to stay alive. This prompted the tree to commit suicide and dry up.

Jesus then replied Peter by saying have *"Have faith in God"*. If faith is built on understanding, then Jesus was simply telling them to understand the way things work with God. His belief was simply because he understood how to get the tree to wither away, he knew that the only way was to get the tree to do it by itself so he gave the tree a reason to do that by disconnecting it from its purpose.

However, the next two verses seem to contradict this point that faith is built on understanding, but a closer examination of the verses show very much how faith works with understanding.

Mark 11:23-24 - KJV

23. For verily I say unto you, That whosoever shall say unto this mountain, Be thou removed, and be thou cast into the sea; and shall not doubt in his heart, but shall believe that those things which he saith shall come to pass; he shall have whatsoever he saith.

24. Therefore I say unto you, What things soever ye desire, when ye pray, believe that ye receive them, and ye shall have them.

Verses 23 and 24 can easily be misinterpreted as saying faith is just to say anything and blindly hope or believe that it would happen. If we are to be truthful, we have done this many times and haven't gotten the desired result. Perhaps the misinterpretation of these verses comes from the failure to take note of the word "*this*" in verse 23.

*23. For verily I say unto you, That whosoever shall say unto **this** mountain, Be thou removed, and be thou cast into the sea; and shall not doubt in his heart, but shall believe that those things which he saith shall come to pass; he shall have whatsoever he saith.*

This points out that Jesus was talking about a particular mountain that was in the vicinity of the fig tree and witnessed the fig tree wither away. Thus, what Jesus was saying to his disciples was that now that the mountain has witnessed what has happened to the fig tree, it was easier to move the mountain.

This simply implies that the challenges that a person faces in life are of various difficulties and to be able to apply faith(understanding) to bigger issues, one need to have understand (have faith) on the smaller issues. Many times, many people are busy trying to solve the bigger picture but don't yet understand how to solve the pixels that make up the picture.

There is another part of the bible that support this knowledge that to be able to solve bigger issues, you should first be able to handle smaller issues. If you do not understand how to overcome smaller temptations, you wouldn't be able to overcome bigger temptations.

Luke 16:10 - KJV

10. He that is faithful in that which is least is faithful also in much: and he that is unjust in the least is unjust also in much.

This was a statement also made by Jesus. (remember we have seen that man's faithfulness/righteousness to God is built on understanding). So, will be right to interpret the above verse as he that has understanding in little will have understanding in much. Thus, if there is a big issue your faith hasn't been able to understand, thus there is a smaller issue you will need to understand first just as understanding how to get the fig tree to kill itself now gave way for understanding how to move that mountain. It's all based on understanding how God has provided for the mountain to move just as much as understanding how God had provided for the tree to kill itself.

Thus, when Jesus replied peter "*Have faith in God*" he was simply saying you need to understand God.

The author of the book of Hebrew who defined faith seems to be in line with this way of addressing the topic of faith.

Hebrews 11:3 - KJV

37

3.   Through faith we understand that the worlds were framed by the word of God, so that things which are seen were not made of things which do appear.

This author clearly shows that faith and understanding go together.

FAITH AND MOUNTAINS

There is also another way to examine the relationship between faith and understanding. According to Jesus, you require faith to move mountains.

Matthew 17:20 - KJV

20. And Jesus said unto them, Because of your unbelief: for verily I say unto you, If ye have faith as a grain of mustard seed, ye shall say unto this mountain, Remove hence to yonder place; and it shall remove; and nothing shall be impossible unto you.

This is also confirmed in another verse in the bible that agrees that faith is what is required to move mountains.

1 Corinthians 13:2 - KJV

2.   And though I have the gift of prophecy, and understand all mysteries, and all knowledge; and though I have all faith, so that I could remove mountains, and have not charity, I am nothing.

Mountains are used in these verses to represent problems and challenges therefore what these verses are saying is that you will require faith to solve problems and tackle challenges. If faith is the same as understanding, these verses are saying that you will require understanding to solve problems and tackle challenges. This we can all agree with. To solve any problem, be it in your job, or family or anywhere, you must have an understanding of the matter at hand.

Many people pray for favour or promotion in their place of work. And because they have sown some sort of seed in church or because they have hope they think they have faith. Meanwhile, their colleagues at work demonstrate a better understanding of the Job, better understanding of the work environment, better understanding of the people they report to, or better understanding of the customers. By our conclusion on faith, it is the colleagues that have more faith. Thus, the colleagues are more qualified for the said promotion.

Some people may be facing mountains in their marriage and thus they turn to prayers and all sorts of religious actions but they never seek to understand marriage from God's point of view, they never seek to understand their spouse, they never seek to understand the root cause of the problem at hand. They are therefore working without faith but just hope.

Some people walk boldly into business ventures because they have consulted some religious leaders who have prayed for them, or they have sown some religious seeds, or they are banking on their religiousness. But they don't seek to have an understanding of the business, its environment, the economic climate, its potential clients, etc.

What they are working with is hope, not faith. It will be difficult for them to move mountains.

It was those with the understanding that moved mountains in transportation by inventing trains, ships and airplanes. It was understanding that moved mountains and brought about electricity and many inventions. To move an actual mountain would only be made possible by understanding (faith).

Only a person with understanding can predict events, especially economic events and plan towards them. And when good things happen easily for such a person, he or she can boldly say he took actions by faith.

Some people are claiming to have faith in the area of marriage but lack understanding of God's view on marriage and how to spot the right person for them. They don't even understand their self so can't even tell who is good for them. So, if God puts the right person in front of them, they might not know it. Yet they would say they have faith. A lot of the mistakes made in life is just down to a lack of understanding (faith).

Some people are believing God for wealth but are not seeking to understand God's principles for wealth. They don't read any books on wealth nor even study wealthy characters in their bible or real life. They have little understanding of wealth yet they claim to have faith that they will be wealthy. Faith can't work without understanding.

It is hard for anyone searching for wealth without understanding to trust his/her process thus when any trial or test arises, they will shake and try to help themselves out by either committing a crime or looking for a shortcut to wealth. It will be hard for such a person to uphold their righteousness in the face of temptation.

Even the idea of praying with faith is better understood when you swap faith for understanding. This becomes praying with understanding. Your prayer request becomes more specific and calculated. You wouldn't be praying amiss. This way it is easier to tell when God is answering your prayer. Also, if you are a man/woman of understanding, you are most likely going to have played your part in getting what you want, therefore you would be praying about things that are beyond your capacity to deliver. This is the area for God to deliver. It is exactly what is meant by doing your best and leaving the rest.

44

ABEL AND FAITH

In Hebrews 11:4 it is said that Abel was able to please God with his offering because of faith.

Hebrews 11:4 – KJV

4. By faith Abel offered unto God a more excellent sacrifice than Cain, by which he obtained witness that he was righteous, God testifying of his gifts: and by it he being dead yet speaketh.

Let us analyse the story of Cain and Abel to see if there was an element of understanding on the part of Abel that could solidify our connection between faith and understanding.

Genesis 4:4-7 - KJV

4.   And Abel, he also brought of the firstlings of his flock and of the fat thereof. And the LORD had respect unto Abel and to his offering:

5.   But unto Cain and to his offering he had not respect. And Cain was very wroth, and his countenance fell.

6.   And the LORD said unto Cain, Why art thou wroth? and why is thy countenance fallen?

7.   If thou doest well, shalt thou not be accepted? and if thou doest not well, sin lieth at the door. And unto thee shall be his desire, and thou shalt rule over him.

There is one important thing in this story that I would like you to take note of, and that is the fact that God rejected Cain even before his offering. In verse seven God clearly stated that it was Cain he did not accept because there was sin at his door.

In the case of Abel also, God had respect for Abel even before his offering.

This means that the acceptance of their offerings was not based on the offering but was based on them. This is what Jesus was talking about in Matthew 5:23.

Matthew 5:23-24 - KJV

23.   Therefore if thou bring thy gift to the altar, and there rememberest that thy brother hath ought against thee;

24.   Leave there thy gift before the altar, and go thy way; first be reconciled to thy brother, and then come and offer thy gift.

Abel must have understood this principle because he was accepted and his offering along with him.

Abel must have checked himself and made sure he was acceptable to God before he offered his offering, he must have understood that it wasn't about the offering but about him, this understanding was counted as faith on the part of Abel

.

FINDING FAITH

Romans 10:17 - KJV

17.   So then faith cometh by hearing, and hearing by the word of God.

This passage shows that faith is gotten by hearing the true word of God.

I have added the word TRUE for a reason. But how can one tell when they are listening to the true word of God?

Psalms 119:130 - KJV

130.   The entrance of thy words giveth light; it giveth understanding unto the simple.

The word of God also brings understanding. This is how you can identify the true word of God.

Many times, what we have been taught in churches and religious houses have not made us understand God any better, they are just doctrines coined by humans.

If a message does not bring understanding, it is not the word of God and thus it can't bring faith.

Perhaps the main takeaway from the two passages above is that both Faith and Understanding have the same source "THE WORD OF GOD".

This further supports the idea that Faith = Understanding.

BUILDING FAITH

We have already established that faith comes through the word of God.

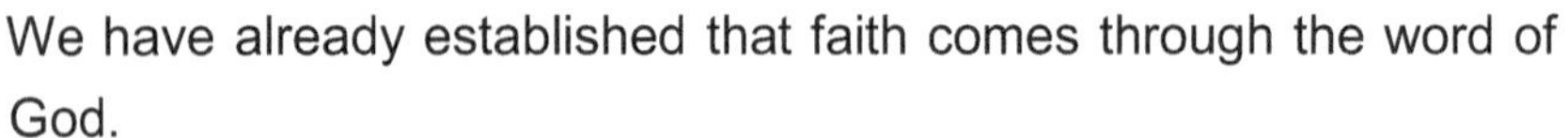

Romans 10:17 - KJV

17. So then faith cometh by hearing, and hearing by the word of God.

But the challenge with many people is that they have failed to realise that the word of God doesn't only come from pastors or via religion.

Anything true can be said to be the word of God. Because the word of God is described as the truth.

John 17:17 - KJV

17.   Sanctify them through thy truth: **thy word is truth.**

Anything that is the truth will lead to understanding.

Psalms 119:130 - KJV

130.   The entrance of thy words giveth light; it giveth understanding unto the simple.

The truth can come from anywhere. It can be your doctor, your friend, anywhere. But the litmus test for the truth is that it will give more understanding of the situation.

A doctor who gives you information about your body that is true is also giving you the word of God. A media house that gives you true information is also giving you the word of God. But with so much information that you can come across, one sure way to identify the truth is that it increases understanding (faith).

I am saying that the way to increase faith is to prioritise knowledge but not all knowledge only those that will increase your understanding. This means that you must in the first place be seeking to understand.

You must be actively seeking to know more and understand more at every time.

The truth is understanding comes from God but without an arsenal of knowledge, there is little for God to work within your life. It is the knowledge that you have that God will use to give you understanding by shedding his light on that knowledge.

If you do not have information/knowledge on the human body, God can't help you understand the human body.

If you do not have information about computers, you can't understand computers. If you are not informed about politics and economics, you can't get to understand politics and the economy. So, understanding starts with knowledge.

It is what you know that God will use to teach you deeper things. If you do not speak English God can't use English to teach you. He will use whatever language you know. God couldn't have used aeroplanes to talk to Moses because Moses did not know what an aeroplane is. So, your understanding/faith is limited by the depth of your knowledge. Without reading and knowing the text in the bible, you would never be able to understand it. So first you would need to know what is written in the bible.

Although there are those who know almost all the text in the bible but do not understand it. This is because they are not open to understanding it.

This leads us to a key ingredient of building faith/understanding which is humility. Without being humble it is difficult to admit within oneself that there could be more to understand in an issue. Many people read the bible and conclude that whatever they conclude has to be the interpretation or whatever interpretation they got from their religious leader is the right interpretation. It takes humility to stay open to anything that could contradict your view provided it increases your level of understanding. But many minds are closed thus they have knowledge but lack understanding.

This is why David said that understanding is given only to the simple (humble).

Psalms 119:130 - KJV

130.   The entrance of thy words giveth light; it giveth understanding unto the simple.

Thus, you can't build your faith without being humble.

The conclusion here is that to be a man/woman of faith you must be hungry for knowledge not only from the bible and you must have a humble spirit. Having knowledge outside of your religion is very vital because most times, God will use your general knowledge to help you understand your religious knowledge. Just the way Jesus used to use his knowledge on farming, politics and other topics as parables when explaining spiritual things.

Having knowledge is the fundamental thing in life, it then gives you room to have understanding and thus increases your faith which will help you be more righteous and overcome mountains/obstacles in life. This will save you from both spiritual and physical destruction of many sorts.

Hosea 4:6 - KJV

6. My people are destroyed for lack of knowledge: because thou hast rejected knowledge, I will also reject thee, that thou shalt be no priest to me: seeing thou hast forgotten the law of thy God, I will also forget thy children.

Unfortunately, many have been fooled to believe that ignorance is bliss.

OLD & NEW TESTAMENTS

This chapter is just to show you that there is no difference between Faith and Understanding. Faith is just mostly used in the New Testament while Understanding was what was commonly used in the old testament. By understanding the way they both work, you would know that they are the same things.

The word "FAITH" appears twice in the old testament that is if we do not count words like faithful or faithfully.

Deuteronomy 32:20 - KJV

20. And he said, I will hide my face from them, I will see what their end shall be: for they are a very froward generation, children in whom is no faith.

Habakkuk 2:4 - KJV

4.   Behold, his soul which is lifted up is not upright in him: but the just shall live by his faith.

The first verse is even consistent with the narrative that lack of faith will lead to displeasing God. While the second verse says a just(righteous) man lives by faith. Both are saying the same thing as the book of Hebrew.

Hebrew 11:6 - KJV

6.   But without faith it is impossible to please him: for he that cometh to God must believe that he is, and that he is a rewarder of them that diligently seek him.

In the new testament, understanding appears a couple of times but is used on one occasion to show that it will help a person grow more in righteousness. Just as David said in the book of Psalms

1 Corinthians 14:20 - KJV

20. Brethren, be not children in understanding: howbeit in malice be ye children, but in understanding be men.

Psalms 111:10 - KJV

*10. The fear of the LORD is the beginning of wisdom: a good **understanding** have all they that do his commandments: his praise endureth for ever.*

Psalms 119:34 - KJV

*34. Give me **understanding**, and I shall keep thy law; yea, I shall observe it with my whole heart.*

GOD'S FAITHFULNESS

Faithfulness is synonymous with the words loyal, correctness, accuracy. In Christianity God's faithfulness is used to indicate that God will always be loyal to his promises and deliver with correctness and accuracy.

But the question is how does God manage to stay faithful to a fault. The answer is understanding. God can deliver anything he wants to deliver because he has the understanding of how to get it done. He knows how to push one man's button for him to meet the need of another man who he wants to bless. He understands all of nature thus he knows how to get them to do his will. God's faithfulness is because he is the source of all understanding.

A closer look at the word faithfulness in the old testament would show it is related or based on understanding.

Numbers 12:7 - KJV

7.   My servant Moses is not so, who is faithful in all mine house.

Here the word faithful is used in place of the word righteous to describe Moses. And according to David, only a man of understanding can stay righteous.

The same use of the word faithful is repeated in the following verses.

1 Samuel 2:35 - KJV

35. And I will raise me up a faithful priest, that shall do according to that which is in mine heart and in my mind: and I will build him a sure house; and he shall walk before mine anointed forever.

2 Kings 12:15 - KJV

15.   Moreover they reckoned not with the men, into whose hand they delivered the money to be bestowed on workmen: for they dealt faithfully.

Nehemiah 7:2 - KJV

2.   That I gave my brother Hanani, and Hananiah the ruler of the palace, charge over Jerusalem: for he was a faithful man, and feared God above many.

Psalms 5:9 - KJV

9.   For there is no faithfulness in their mouth; their inward part is very wickedness; their throat is an open sepulchre; they flatter with their tongue.

If we keep examining all the verses linked to faithfulness, you would see that you can't be faithful without being righteous and we know that you can't be righteous without having understanding.

Psalms 111:10 – KJV

*10.   The fear of the LORD is the beginning of wisdom: a good **understanding** have all they that do his commandments: his praise endureth for ever.*

Psalms 119:34 – KJV

*34.   Give me **understanding,** and I shall keep thy law; yea, I shall observe it with my whole heart.*

Thus, to be faithful (full of faith/ full of complete confidence) is to be full of understanding or full of righteousness.

Many Christians have been working with the mindset that faith is just to believe that something would happen. When their hopes or expectations are not met, they begin to doubt God not realizing that they haven't understood the way faith works. They haven't understood that faith can't exist without understanding and what they need is to understand God. Any man who was described to have worked by faith in the bible must also have been righteous therefore a man of understanding

FAITH AND TEMPTATION

Without faith, it is impossible to please God. An integral part of pleasing God is being able to overcome temptations. Since we are saying that faith is built on understanding, then it means you require understanding to overcome temptations.

Let us examine the very first temptation in the bible (the temptation of Eve) and see if an understanding could have helped.

Genesis 3:1-7 - KJV

1.   Now the serpent was more subtle than any beast of the field which the LORD God had made. And he said unto the woman, Yea, hath God said, Ye shall not eat of every tree of the garden?

2.   And the woman said unto the serpent, We may eat of the fruit of the trees of the garden:

3.   But of the fruit of the tree which is in the midst of the garden, God hath said, Ye shall not eat of it, neither shall ye touch it, lest ye die.

4.   And the serpent said unto the woman, Ye shall not surely die:

5.   For God doth know that in the day ye eat thereof, then your eyes shall be opened, and ye shall be as gods, knowing good and evil.

6.   And when the woman saw that the tree was good for food, and that it was pleasant to the eyes, and a tree to be desired to make one wise, she took of the fruit thereof, and did eat, and gave also unto her husband with her; and he did eat.

7.   And the eyes of them both were opened, and they knew that they were naked; and they sewed fig leaves together, and made themselves aprons.

In this temptation, all the serpent did was trick the woman that if she eats from the tree of knowledge of good and evil, she will be like gods (verse 5). But this was a trick because there was no need for Eve to want to be like gods. After all, in chapter one of Genesis, it is said that she was already created in the image of the almighty God. But the serpent was able to paint becoming a god (take note of the small letter g) as a step forward for Eve.

Genesis 1:27 – KJV

*27.   So God **created** man in his own image, in the image of God created he him; male and female created he them.*

The only reason why Eve fell for this is that she was ignorant to the fact that she was already in the image of the almighty God. At the time God decided to create man in His image, man was not in existence thus the only beings that knew that man was created in the image of God are whoever God was speaking to in Genesis 1:26.

Genesis 1:26 – KJV

26.   And God said, Let us make man in our image, after our likeness: and let them have dominion over the fish of the sea, and over the fowl of the air, and over the cattle, and over all the earth, and over every creeping thing that creepeth upon the earth.

Let's assume that Eve had already been told that she was created in the image of God, she could still have fallen for the temptation because there is a difference between knowing and understanding.

So perhaps Eve did not understand how she was created in the image of God.

Many of us still lack this understanding to this day. Whenever we hear that we are created in the image of God, we automatically think that God looks physically the way we do. But that would be wrong considering that there are many imperfections in our physical body. God can't be said to have such imperfections.

So how then are we created in the image of God?

To understand this, we have to know what the image of God is.

John 4:24 - KJV

*24.   God is a **Spirit:** and they that worship him must worship him in spirit and in truth.*

God is a spirit, this is why no one has seen God physically therefore if man was created in the image of God, then man had to have been a spirit. Only that man was given a body in Genesis 2:7.

Genesis 2:6-7 - KJV

*6.	But there went up a **mist** from the earth, and **watered** the whole face of the **ground.***

*7.	And the LORD God formed man of the dust of the ground, and breathed into his nostrils the breath of life; and man became a living soul.*

So, the serpent was only able to get Eve because Eve did not understand how she was created in the image of God. That it was a spiritual resemblance to God not physical. If she had thought that her resemblance to God was physical then that explains why it was easy to convince her that that wasn't enough because when it comes to our physical body, there are too many flaws and limitations to be able to prove that we are in the image of God.

This is why even to this day many Christians struggle to have complete confidence (faith) that they are in the image of God because they do not understand that it is not a physical image but spiritual. We do not understand that Man is a spiritual being like God only that man is housed in a physical container called the flesh. Many people do not understand that we are not our flesh.

Eve's faith failed because she lacked understanding. This shows that there is no faith without understanding.

Another example of temptation is the one joseph faced in the house of Potiphar. Potiphar's wife tried to seduce Joseph into sexual immorality but Joseph ran away even leaving his garment behind.

Genesis 39:7 - 12 - KJV

7.   And it came to pass after these things, that his master's wife cast her eyes upon Joseph; and she said, Lie with me.

8.   But he refused, and said unto his master's wife, Behold, my master wotteth not what is with me in the house, and he hath committed all that he hath to my hand;

9.   There is none greater in this house than I; neither hath he kept back any thing from me but thee, because thou art his wife: how then can I do this great wickedness, and sin against God?

10.   And it came to pass, as she spake to Joseph day by day, that he hearkened not unto her, to lie by her, or to be with her.

11.   And it came to pass about this time, that Joseph went into the house to do his business; and there was none of the men of the house there within.

12.   And she caught him by his garment, saying, Lie with me: and he left his garment in her hand, and fled, and got him out.

What saved Joseph in this temptation was that he understood that when it comes to sexual urges, the surest way to overcome is to flee(run). Don't even think about trusting your flesh in such situations, run while you still have the will to.

1 Corinthians 6:18 - KJV

18.   Flee fornication. Every sin that a man doeth is without the body; but he that committeth fornication sinneth against his own body.

2 Timothy 2:22 - KJV

22.   Flee   also   youthful   lusts: but   follow righteousness, faith, charity, peace, with them that call on the Lord out of a pure heart.

Unfortunately, many people do not understand this rule. They constantly stick around sexual temptations, trusting that they can handle them until they fall and start regretting their decisions.

Jesus was another person who used understanding(faith) to overcome temptation. His understanding of the scriptures he had read, and his understanding of what is important in life was what he used to overcome his temptations.

Matthew 4:1-10 - KJV

1.   Then was Jesus led up of the Spirit into the wilderness to be tempted of the devil.

2.   And when he had fasted forty days and forty nights, he was afterward an hungred.

3.   And when the tempter came to him, he said, If thou be the Son of God, command that these stones be made bread.

4.	But he answered and said, It is written, Man shall not live by bread alone, but by every word that proceedeth out of the mouth of God.

5.	Then the devil taketh him up into the holy city, and setteth him on a pinnacle of the temple,

6.	And saith unto him, If thou be the Son of God, cast thyself down: for it is written, He shall give his angels charge concerning thee: and in their hands they shall bear thee up, lest at any time thou dash thy foot against a stone.

7.	Jesus said unto him, It is written again, Thou shalt not tempt the Lord thy God.

8.	Again, the devil taketh him up into an exceeding high mountain, and sheweth him all the kingdoms of the world, and the glory of them;

9.	And saith unto him, All these things will I give thee, if thou wilt fall down and worship me.

10.	Then saith Jesus unto him, Get thee hence, Satan: for it is written, Thou shalt worship the Lord thy God, and him only shalt thou serve.

Most temptations occur like arguments or debates either in your head or with someone else. And if you lack knowledge and understanding, it is very difficult to win these debates. Thus, your faith is most likely going to fail in such a situation. So, we can see that faith and righteousness both rely on Understanding. Thus, the three are inseparable.

The book of ephesians chapter 6 describes faith as a shield that can help protect from temptations or any tricks played on our minds.

Ephesians 6:16 - KJV

16. Above all, taking the shield of faith, wherewith ye shall be able to quench all the fiery darts of the wicked.

Here the phrase fiery darts of the wicked is used to depict temptations, doubts, fears and many tricky tools the devil(wicked) tries to use to get us to fall and do something wrong or to make mistakes. This verse simply says that our first line of defence should be faith. If faith is understanding, therefore our shield against the tricks of the wicked(devil), is faith.

FAITH WITHOUT WORK

James 2:26 - KJV

26.   For as the body without the spirit is dead, so faith without works is dead also.

This can also be interpreted to say that understanding without application is dead (waste).

After getting an understanding, you must consciously fight to apply it in your life or there will be no point in getting the understanding in the first place.

James 2:17-24 - KJV

17. Even so faith, if it hath not works, is dead, being alone.

18. Yea, a man may say, Thou hast faith, and I have works: shew me thy faith without thy works, and I will shew thee my faith by my works.

20. But wilt thou know, O vain man, that faith without works is dead?

22. Seest thou how faith wrought with his works, and by works was faith made perfect?

24. Ye see then how that by works a man is justified, and not by faith only.

There is no point in thirsting for knowledge and seeking understanding and claiming to have faith but you don't allow your understanding to reflect in your actions.

Working by understanding is the definition of working in faith.

84

SUMMARY

The summary of this book is simple, faith can't exist without understanding. So, it is advisable that when you read the bible, anytime you come across the word faith, you replace it with understanding and see how you begin to get the deeper pictures of most of the bible. Faith can either be replaced with Understanding or Righteousness, they are fundamentally the same.

A good example to use for this will be Hebrew 12:2

Hebrew 12:2 - KJV

2.   Looking unto Jesus the author and finisher of our faith; who for the joy that was set before him endured the cross, despising the shame, and is set down at the right hand of the throne of God.

This can be translated as "looking unto Jesus, the author and finisher of our understanding". Indirectly saying that everything a Christian should believe and seek to understand can be found within the teachings of Jesus.

But like I said, there are many things that a man can seek to understand in life. What will happen is that God will use these things to shed light on core spiritual issues.

What I am ultimately saying is that the ultimate thing an individual need to be able to navigate this life is understanding.

Proverb 4:7 - KJV

7.   Wisdom is the principal thing; therefore get wisdom: and with all thy getting get understanding.

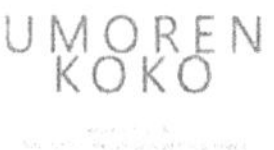
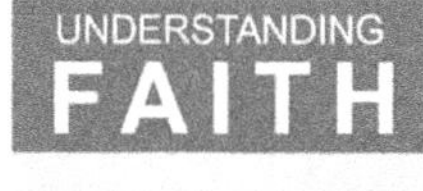

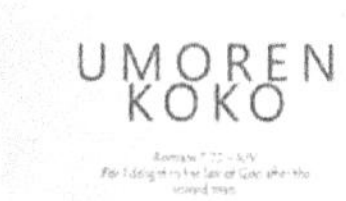

THE
FREEDOM
SERIES

This is a series of five
books designed to
free
your soul from the
control of the flesh
and the mindset of

sin.

Umoren Koko is a life coach, a teacher and an economist born in the city of Lagos in Nigeria. He has a first degree in Economics from Covenant University in Nigeria. He also has a Masters Degree in International Business And Management from Nottingham Trent University.
Motivated by the quest to understand life with the aim of helping people live a much simpler and fulfilling life, Koko has spent most of his adult years seeking to understand God and his ways so that he can be a medium for educating people on the things of God and Life.

This is the first book of the freedom series; a series of five books designed to make your soul free from the control of the flesh and the mindset of sin.

UNDERSTANDING
FAITH